DISCOVER DOGS WITH THE AMERICAN CANINE ASSOCIATION

I LIKE PUGS!

Linda Bozzo

It is the Mission of the American Canine Association (ACA) to provide registered dog owners with the educational support needed for raising, training, showing, and breeding the healthiest pets expected by responsible pet owners throughout the world. Through our activities and services, we encourage and support the dog world in order to promote best-known husbandry standards as well as to ensure that the voice and needs of our customers are quickly and properly addressed.

Our continued support, commitment, and direction are guided by our customers, including veterinary, legal, and legislative advisors. ACA aims to provide the most efficient, cooperative, and courteous service to our customers and strives to set the standard for education and problem solving for all who depend on our services.

For more information, please visit www.acacanines.com, e-mail customerservice@acadogs.com, phone 1-800-651-8332, or write to the American Canine Association at PO Box 121107, Clermont, FL 34712.

Published in 2017 by Enslow Publishing, LLC.
101 W. 23rd Street, Suite 240, New York, NY 10011
Copyright © 2017 by Enslow Publishing, LLC.
All rights reserved.
No part of this book may be reproduced by any means without the written permission of the publisher.

Library of Congress Cataloging-in-Publication Data
Names: Bozzo, Linda.
Title: I like pugs! / Linda Bozzo.
Description: New York, NY : Enslow Publishing, 2017. | Series: Discover dogs with the American Canine Association | Includes bibliographical references and index. | Audience: Ages 5 and up. | Audience: Grades K to 3.
Identifiers: LCCN 2015046917| ISBN 9780766077874 (library bound) | ISBN 9780766078024 (pbk.) | ISBN 9780766077676 (6-pack)
Subjects: LCSH: Pug--Juvenile literature.
Classification: LCC SF429.P9 B69 2016 | DDC 636.76--dc23
LC record available at http://lccn.loc.gov/2015046917

Printed in Malaysia.

To Our Readers: We have done our best to make sure all website addresses in this book were active and appropriate when we went to press. However, the author and the publisher have no control over and assume no liability for the material available on those websites or on any websites they may link to. Any comments or suggestions can be sent by e-mail to customerservice@enslow.com.

Photo Credits: Cover, p. 1 Ermolaev Alexander/Shutterstock.com; p. 3 Nature Art/Shutterstock.com (left), fabio camandona/Shutterstock.com (right); p. 5 XiXinXing/Thinkstock; p. 6 Eric Isselee/Shutterstock.com; p. 9 Jesse Kunerth/ Thinkstock; p. 10 Oleg/Shutterstock.com; p. 11 Timolina/Shutterstock.com; p. 13 Dora Zett/Shutterstock.com (pug eating), jclegg/Shutterstock.com (collar), Luisa Leal Photography (bed), gvictoria/Shutterstock.com (brush), In-Finity/Shutterstock.com (dishes), iStock.com/Lisa Thornberg (leash, toys); p. 14 Ron Chappie Stock/Thinkstock; p 14 iStock.com/Pamela Moore (top), Valerio Pardi/Shutterstock.com (bottom); p. 15 Tannis Toohey/Toronto Star/Getty Images; p. 17 Ezzolo/Shutterstock.com; p. 18 iStock.com/bernardbodo; p. 19 BrandXPictures/Thinkstock; p. 21 iStock.com/Grace Butler; p. 22 gp88/Shutterstock.com.

Enslow Publishing
101 W. 23rd Street
Suite 240
New York, NY 10011
USA
enslow.com

TINLEY PARK PUBLIC LIBRARY

CONTENTS

IS A PUG RIGHT FOR YOU? 4

A DOG OR A PUPPY? 7

LOVING YOUR PUG 8

EXERCISE 11

FEEDING YOUR PUG 12

GROOMING 15

WHAT YOU SHOULD KNOW 16

A GOOD FRIEND 19

NOTE TO PARENTS 20

WORDS TO KNOW 22

READ ABOUT DOGS (BOOKS AND WEBSITES) 23

INDEX 24

IS A PUG RIGHT FOR YOU?

Pugs make great family pets. They are happy living in the country or the city. Pugs enjoy being with children and older adults. This breed gets along with other pets but does not mind being the only dog.

A DOG OR A PUPPY?

Training a young pug takes time, but it is a must. If you do not have time to train a puppy, an older pug may be better for your family.

Pugs grow to be small in size, 13–20 pounds (6–9 kilograms).

LOVING YOUR PUG

With those big eyes, curly tails, and wrinkly faces, pugs are easy to love. Love your pug, and he will love you in return.

EXERCISE

Your pug will need walks on a **leash** every day. Pugs are also very playful. Your pug will always be ready to play games, like **fetch**, with you.

FAST FACT: Pugs do not do well in the heat. On hot days, walks should be kept short.

FEEDING YOUR PUG

Pugs love to eat, but they only need a small amount of food. Dogs can be fed wet or dry dog food. Ask a **veterinarian** (vet), a doctor for animals, which food is best for your dog and how much to feed her.

Give your pug fresh, clean water every day.

Remember to keep your dog's food and water dishes clean. Dirty dishes can make a dog sick.

Do not feed your dog people food.
It can make her sick.

Your new dog will need:

a collar with a tag

a bed

a brush

food and water dishes

a leash

toys

Food and dirt can get trapped in a pug's wrinkles. Keep dog wipes handy to clean them.

GROOMING

Pugs **shed**, which means their hair falls out. They should be brushed at least once a week. A pug's face wrinkles need to be cleaned regularly.

Use a gentle soap made just for dogs.

Your pug will need a bath every so often. His nails need to be clipped. A vet or **groomer** can show you how. Your dog's ears should be cleaned, and his teeth should be brushed by an adult.

WHAT YOU SHOULD KNOW

Pugs make good watchdogs. They bark at any sign of trouble.

The pug's eyes can be easily injured.

Because of their flat face, pugs have trouble breathing.

Pugs love to clown around and show off.

You will need to take your new dog to the vet for a checkup. He will need shots, called vaccinations, and yearly checkups to keep him healthy. If you think your dog may be sick, call your vet.

A GOOD FRIEND

Pugs can live around 12 to 15 years. Like a good friend, your pug will love to always be by your side.

NOTE TO PARENTS

It is important to consider having your dog spayed or neutered when the dog is young. Spaying and neutering are operations that prevent unwanted puppies and can help improve the overall health of your dog.

It is also a good idea to microchip your dog, in case he or she gets lost. A vet will implant a painless microchip under the skin, which can then be scanned at a vet's office or animal shelter to look up your information on a national database.

Some towns require licenses for dogs, so be sure to check with your town clerk.

For more information, speak with a vet.

There are many dogs, young and old, waiting to be adopted from animal shelters and rescue groups.

Words to Know

fetch – To go after a toy and bring it back.

groomer – A person who bathes and brushes dogs.

leash – A chain or strap that attaches to the dog's collar.

shed – When dog hair falls out so new hair can grow.

vaccinations – Shots that dogs need to stay healthy.

veterinarian (vet) – A doctor for animals.

Read About Dogs

Books

Barnes, Nico. *Pugs*. Minneapolis, MN: Abdo Kids, 2015.

Landau, Elaine. *Pugs Are the Best*. Minneapolis, MN: Lerner Publications, 2011.

Websites

American Canine Association Inc., Kids Corner
acakids.com/

National Geographic for Kids, Pet Central
kids.nationalgeographic.com/explore/pet-central/

PBS Kids, Dog Games
pbskids.org/games/dog

INDEX

A
animal shelters, 20, 21

B
bathing, 15
beds for dogs, 13
breathing in pugs, 16
brushing, 13, 15

C
children and pugs, 4
city, pugs in, 4
collars for dogs, 13
country, pugs in, 4

D
dishes for dogs, 12, 13

E
exercise, 11

F
feeding, 12, 13

G
games, 11
grooming, 15

I
injury in pugs, 16
items needed for dogs, 13

L
leashes, 11, 13
licenses for dogs, 20
lifespan of pugs, 19

M
microchips, 20

N
nail clipping, 15

O
other pets and pugs, 4

P
personality of pugs, 4, 16
puppies, 7, 20

S
size of pugs, 7
spaying/neutering, 20

T
tags for dogs, 13
toys for dogs, 13
training, 7

V
vaccinations, 18
veterinarians, 12, 15, 18, 20

W
walks, 11
watchdogs, 16
water, 12, 13
weather needed for pugs, 11
wrinkles of pugs, 14, 15